# Getting Past GateKeepers

B. Vincent

Published by RWG Publishing, 2021.

GETTING PAST GATEKEEPERS

**First edition. June 14, 2021.**

Written by B. Vincent.

# Also by B. Vincent

**Affiliate Marketing**
Affiliate Marketing

**Standalone**
Affiliate Recruiting
Business Layoffs & Firings
Business and Entrepreneur Guide
Business Remote Workforce
Career Transition
Project Management
Precision Targeting
Professional Development
Strategic Planning
Content Marketing
Imminent List Building
Getting Past GateKeepers

# Table of Contents

# Getting Past GateKeepers

Hello and welcome to this course on getting past the gatekeeper. In this course, we'll show you how to reach more decision-makers with your b2b sales calls. This course is divided into three modules, modules one and two will give you a brief overview of gatekeepers and useful methods and tactics for getting past them, and module three goes over pre-call intelligence gathering, by the time this course is over, you'll be equipped with the tools and methods you need to get past gatekeepers, so you can make more sales. So, without further ado, let's dive into the first module. Okay guys, welcome to module one. In this module, our trainer will give you a brief overview of gatekeepers and some ideas of how to get past them, so get ready to take some notes, and let's jump right in.

# Module 1

The dreaded gatekeeper has been a part of the cold calling game for decades. Sales professionals have spent their careers trying to develop and fine-tune different tactics for getting past these b2b guardians and through to the decision-makers, so they can book appointments, and make sales. A gatekeeper is someone whose job it is, to keep you away from the person you're trying to reach. Typically, there is a receptionist, secretary, or executive assistant, although that's not always the case. They man the phones, they take incoming calls, they assess those calls to determine whether they're important or legitimate expected calls, and they filter out the calls that they think the decision-maker won't want to be bothered with. They know you're out there. They've been warned, trained even coached to look for telltale signs of cold calling salespeople. They've been lied to, tricked made to look like fools around the office by some cold callers and many of them regularly lie themselves too, although it's usually to say someone who's in a meeting or not in the office. For most of them, it's not their first rodeo. They're ready for you, and with every passing year, they're getting smarter, savvier, and better at their job, which is why you and your business need to stay on the cutting edge of this concept as well.

Let's go over some ways you can do that. So, for starters, remember what your parents tell you. And what I mean is just use basic manners, make sure you're saying please make sure you're saying thank you. Make sure you're using emphatic versions of those, like, thanks so much for your help and so on and so forth. Be nice, you have to keep in mind that the gatekeeper is someone who the company likes, that's why they're in that position. They wouldn't be manning the phones if the company didn't like him or her. Does that kind of make sense? If they're sitting there at the counter and they've had that job, clearly the decision-maker that you want to work with, whose good side you want to be on, likes this person, enough to keep her or him there in that position. So, the last thing you want to do is be on bad terms with someone who everybody in the office likes. And the very last thing you want to do is end up on the blacklist for being rude or impatient, social bonds and camaraderie, all that's really very real, in an office environment. And in many cases that will override profit, which means no matter how cool what you're selling is, they'll choose not to do business with you if they had the impression that you were not respecting one of their valued team members.

Next, use first names, and that includes there's, not just the executives. So, if you call in, and the gatekeeper says this is Pam, how may I direct your call. Your first sentence should be, hi Pam, can you put me through to such and such, mentioned the gatekeepers name, this has been proven time and time again, it's not a silver bullet right it's not a skeleton key, it's not going to guarantee that you get through, but it does, and it's been proven, it does have some psychological advantages. So, mention their

first name and use the executives first name, when possible, if you did a good job of collecting that information, to begin with.

Next thing is, understand their perspective. And what I really mean is no kidding, sit down and pretend to do a thought experiment, pretend that you are the gatekeeper at their company, maybe you have a scary boss or an impatient boss. Maybe you have a boss who you really like and respected you're actually motivated to keep the annoying salespeople away from him or her. Maybe you deal with cold callers all day long. Maybe by the time you're calling in, they've already had like 10 cold calls that morning. Maybe you as a gatekeeper remember we're pretending to be in their shoes here. Maybe you deal with people lying all the time, people trying to pull those sly little tricks that you hear about, and you're annoyed by it, understandably. Understand their perspective, so that you'll have that in your back pocket when you call them.

Next, just practice good listening skills. Be a human, when they're speaking, if they're saying things, practice those good active listening skills that we've all learned. If they say oh man, he's really busy now you can say oh yeah, I can imagine I know that guy's busy, or oh you know we've really been swamped because of XYZ recent event, and you can say oh no kidding, wow! Even something as simple as sure, sure, or totally understand being inserted here or there when they're saying things or explaining a situation can go a long way in increasing likeability and making yourself sound much more human.

Next to piggyback on using their name after they've told it to you. Don't just use the sentence during recall, but mark it down, remember it, make a note in your CRM for when you call them again. Because if you call them and you're immediately using their name, or if you're reaching out via email and using their name. Again, it establishes you as an actual fellow human being. It has a positive psychological effect on the whole thing. So, keep that in mind, put it down in your CRM that name should be as important to you, as the name of the executive you're trying to reach as far as the intelligence gathering and putting the information into your CRM.

Next, make sure you end on a positive note, no matter what happened, and what that means is, even if you didn't have success you didn't get through the decision-maker, he got kicked back or rejected again. Don't let those emotions show in your voice. You have to mask that and end on a very positive and appreciative note, oh, that's too bad, or I'll try some other time, thanks so much for your time, have a great rest of your day. Make sure it's a positive tone and a positive message when you end because guess what you're going to have to be dealing with that gatekeeper again. And you want to make sure you maintain the positivity in that relationship between you and them.

Next, and this is kind of outside the box thing and it might actually be a little bit cliche. If you use it in the wrong situation, but if you actually spent a little bit of time on the phone with the gatekeeper. You know you established a connection and they tried to help you reach so and so or gave you some info on this or that it wouldn't hurt, to send them a little thank you card. Even a thank-you email but a thank you card would be really classy. Again, don't send them a thank you card if all you had was like a two-sentence conversation because it'll seem pretentious, you want to avoid being pretentious. And that actually applies to a lot of things that we're going to learn that can be really good tactics for getting past gatekeepers. But if you're not really careful with how and when you use them, it can come off as pretentious, or disingenuous. Okay, but this if the circumstances call for it and your gut tell you that this would be a good idea, go ahead and send a thank you card, because then your name will be more memorable to them, okay, and they're more likely to pay a little bit more attention to you when you call or follow up in the future. So, all of these have been pretty basic points, right pretty elementary, there are no ninja hacks shared yet. We just wanted to cover the basics here so you're prepared mentally, and when you start your cold calling, this is sort of the basic one on one level foundation that everybody should have in the next lesson, we'll cover some more advanced tips and tricks for getting past the gatekeeper.

# Module 2

Hey folks, welcome to module two. In this module, our trainer will cover even more methods and tactics for getting past the gatekeeper, so get ready to take some notes, and let's jump right in.

So, one of the most important things you can do, when trying to get past the gatekeeper, is different. Be different, you have to understand that from the gatekeeper's perspective they have a very clear pattern, a very clear routine that they go through, it's a cycle, right. They answer the phone, they ask why the person is calling. They listened to the explanation of why they're calling. They say that the decision-maker is busy, whether it's true or not, what's usually probably true, right, and then they get rid of the salesperson, they get rid of your pesky cold caller, that's their routine. Figure out who it is and why they're calling, listen to the explanation, say that the person is too busy, get rid of the cold caller. That's their pattern, and the only way you're going to get out of that pattern which I assure you they go through all the times it's not their first rodeo. The only way is through differentiation, you have to be different somehow. And there's no one specific way to do that, there's a bunch of things that you can do to be a little bit different.

And we'll cover some of those throughout the rest of this lesson. One thing that you might want to consider is to do a little bit of research about something specific about the company, that you know is ongoing at the moment, like a strategic initiative, or you know, the fact that maybe they just recently opened up an office and expanded into another area so they're likely to have a need for this or that service or the fact that they're in the market for a certain type of solution, or maybe even bad news recently, but be careful with the bad news, be careful with bringing that up. But if it's something recently, and you can say hey is Jim there, I want to talk to him about, you know such and such initiative, or hey is Bob there, I heard you guys are expanding into such and such neighborhood, and I wanted to talk to him about how we can help do that, you know, something along those lines. If you have those types of little factoids, that the gatekeeper will know about, and they will appreciate that you know about them because it differentiates you a little bit. Well, then you should, mathematically, get better results, overall, if you can insert something along those lines. And that all comes down to research before starting to call. Something kind of similar is to send some type of communication to the decision-maker, in advance whether it be via LinkedIn message or an email, or an envelope that you sent into the office. So that then when they pick up the phone and ask what this is about, you could say, well I'm following up on such and such proposal, where I'm following up on such and such, you know issue, right, or the thing that I sent him. Right, that just in and of itself, sort of sets you apart and differentiates you a little bit because it sounds in the gatekeepers mind, potentially, that there's already some type of business going on between you and the decision-maker, and that therefore the decision-maker would want to hear what you have to say.

Now here's another tactic that people don't often think about, which is kind of the same, but it's in reverse. Instead of you having sent something proactively to the decision-maker, the decision-maker requested something from you. Now what do we mean by that, or we're talking about those situations where you have a lead page or an opt-in page with a lead magnet. Right, so if they're on your blog or your website or you sent out, you know ads he did an ad campaign you brought people to a landing page and said Hey if you'd like to learn more about XYZ solution, put in your email address and we'll send you a PDF and so on and so forth. If you have any of those types of things going on in your business. And someone actually requested them even if they didn't put in their phone number, even if it was just an email opt-in form, but you know that the person, the decision-maker themselves did request that information from you, well then it's totally legitimate to say to the gatekeeper, so and so said he was interested in XYZ service or so and so said he wanted to hear more about this or that service. And the gatekeepers mind once again unless you're lying, and they'll always be suspicious that you might be lying because they get lied to by cold callers all the time. But outside of the suspicion that you're lying. They're going to assume hey there's a good chance that this is true, and that Bob really does want to hear from this guy on the phone. Not related to all of this is the next point and that is intelligence collection, you have to collect your intel. You want to know the decision makers' names, okay.

The main one, but then also anyone else in the office, you know, depending on the size of the business that you're cold calling, there might be a few different managers, there might be a few different managing directors, right, a few different executives. And so have names ready have a main guy who you're going through. But it's even better if you have a whole suite of names, and you could say all he's not around, okay, how about Steve is he in. Right, if you have those names and particularly those, those first names, which will give the impression to the gatekeeper that you actually know these people. Well, then you're going to have a much higher chance of success. Same thing goes for numbers if you can collect, not just the main business, I put the actual direct lines to these people, that's huge. If you can get a direct line to the decision-maker's office that's absolutely phenomenal. As long as you use it the right way, use it with care, right. Same thing goes for emails, if you have direct emails they can go to the decision-makers, that's absolutely fantastic. Business hours, as silly as it sounds business hours are very important, not because you want to know about the hours, but because you want to know about the time outside of those hours, because sometimes calling before or after can help you and we'll get to that point a little bit later, but you want to know the business hours.

Now there are companies that sell this information. Okay, there are software as a service solution that you can actually get into and they have a huge database you pay him, you know 100 bucks a month or so, and they have a huge database, of already collected information about decision-makers, and we're talking 10s upon 10s of 1000s of companies all over the United States, maybe even hundreds of 1000s. We're talking a lot of information, we're talking first and last names, and the positions that they hold within the company, and the direct line or the direct email and so on and so forth. This is really valuable information, and it is worth the money that you pay for it.

Now sometimes, it depends on you know how old the information is, maybe it's out of date, but it's better than nothing, it's a good starting point. Right, if you're ever worried about that if you think your data is a little bit old, you can always call the gatekeeper and say hey is Bob still in charge of such and such.

And you get a yes or no from them and then you can mark that down as accurate information or inaccurate information to figure out, you know who actually is the decision-maker that you are going after. And that actually brings us to the next point, and that is, use your gatekeeper conversation as an intelligence-gathering tool. The gatekeeper is not [inaudible 15:46]. It's true you want to just get past them as quickly as possible, if possible. Right, so your initial goal is to get past them right, get through the gatekeeper to the decision-maker, but as soon as you realize that that's not going to happen right away. And that you're going to have to have a little bit of exchange back and forth between you and the gatekeeper. You should immediately switch gears and make that an intelligence-gathering mission. Ask the gatekeeper questions, like we just said a moment ago. Hey, is Bob still in charge of such and such, who's in charge of marketing, who's in charge of sales, right? How many managing directors do you guys have? Hey, what time does Bill come in in the morning? What times does everybody leave? Right, you get this kind of information. And it's in many ways, it's much more valuable than the stuff you would get from one of those databases that you're paying for because you know it's current, it's coming from an actual person who sits right in the middle of the office and knows everything that's going on.

So, the gatekeepers absolutely just incredibly valuable treasure trove of information, and you want to make sure that you use the gatekeeper to that end. One thing you can ask is, what would you say is the best time to call and reach him. What you're doing here is you're setting up, a follow-up, a follow-up. That sounds like a formal meeting, it's not a formal meeting. Okay, but you can sort of pitch it and spin it that way when you call back. Right, so if you can't get through to Bill and Bill is the decision-maker that you're trying to reach. And you say, what would be a good time to call back tomorrow that you might be available what's the best of my day do you think, and they say well yeah, he might be available around nine to 10 in the mornings, usually, that's between his meetings or whatever they tell you, well that's good. That's fantastic, you can pencil that, and you can say hey thanks so much for your time, I'll try and give him a call between those hours. When you call the next day, you can literally say, hey, I was told to give Bill a call right about now, is he available. Right, and so you have a point of reference that you can refer back to, about a previous conversation that you had so it doesn't sound like a cold call anymore.

I mean, it almost sounds like an expected call. The way you kind of spin it, is to give the impression through your tone, that it was almost an appointment, like Bill is expecting you to call, are you were told to call Bill. Right, which is not really stretching the truth at all it's, you asked what's the best time to call, and the gatekeeper gave you a time, so use it that way.

Now one common thing that you might hear from a gatekeeper is. Is Bill expecting your call? Is he expecting you? Or is she expecting you? And you have to know how you're going to answer this, okay. In fact, we'll talk about the common objections filed in a moment. But there's a few things that you can try and they're a little bit tongue in cheek sometimes, sometimes they work sometimes they don't, you want to be cautious. But you could say, oh, I sure hope so. He better be expecting me or something to that effect, especially if you did, in fact, send an email to him previously or they did in fact opt-in to some type of lead opt-in form, to get a PDF or a lead magnet from you. You have just cause for using the phrase I should hope so when they say, is he expecting you.

Another variation of this question is what's this regarding. What's this about? And in those cases, you can either tell them exactly what it's about, you can say, well I want to talk to him about the XYZ issue or such and such initiative or follow up on such and such that I sent him, right. Or you can take kind of a senior steamroller approach, and that is to say, just tell him it's regarding your name, you just say your name. Right, so if your name is John Smith. They say who's speaking, John Smith. What's this regarding? Just tell them it's about John Smith. Surprisingly, there have been salespeople who have used this to great effect if you have the right tone and we'll talk about that in a moment. If you have the right tone that can be very effective. But that's not the only question that you're going to get hit with and it's not the only objection, you're going to get hit with which brings us to our next point and that is, create, and carefully practice answering a common objections file.

As you're going through the cold calling process, you're going to notice that gatekeepers tend to ask the same questions or have the same objections or the same excuses. And you want to know what you're going to say when they say those things, so you don't have to think on your feet. So, if they say, we don't have time for this. What, you want a response to that, you know, maybe it's sort of the car don't agree with everything approach. Right, how yeah no, I totally understand, I agree, you don't have time for this, you guys are busy. So, what would you say is a good time for me to call you back?

Right, or maybe it's a different approach, whatever it is, you need to have it, rehearsed, and practiced, and be ready for that objection. My boss doesn't want to talk with sales reps. That's an objection, they might be blunt and say that. What's your response going to be? There might be tripping all over yourself. And then mumbling and stuttering if you're not prepared for it so be prepared for it. We've tried something like this before, but it didn't work. Well, that might be a common objection. It's possible that the gatekeeper will say that to you, you'd think, you know, maybe the decision-maker would say that, but the gatekeeper might say that especially if they are familiar with what's going on in the company. If they know if you're offering, let's say reputation management services, and the gatekeeper is close with the executives, and he or she knows that they've tried two or three reputation management services in the last couple years, and that didn't work and they've heard the executives complained about it, guess what they might come right out and say that to you. They might already have a verbal or maybe even an unspoken, understanding with the executives, or what they think is an unspoken understanding with the executives, that they're not interested in hearing any more about reputation management. Or whatever service you're offering, so they might say that, and if they say that what are you going to say you have to have a response plan so that it's right there in your pocket you can just pull it out right there on the tip of your tongue.

Just send us some information, that's a common one, just send us an email here. Yeah, we'd love to hear what you have to say, here's our email address, send us some information, which nine times out of 10 means go away. What are you going to say?

It's not a priority right now, that's another one. Have a response for that, have a response for everything that you expect to get, especially the things that you've noticed that you consistently get, from gatekeepers' objections and questions have a response have rehearsed and be ready.

Now we talked a moment ago about what you can say when someone's asking if you're expected or what your call is about. And we talked about the sort of steamroller approach, where you're just going straight through them, saying, I just tell them it's about John Smith. Just tell him it's regarding John Smith or something to that effect.

Now, the only way you're going to nail that and it's going to work is if you have the right type of tone, and the tone has to be senior, not superior. Senior, you want a confident and busy tone, meaning you're a top-level guy you sound like you're an executive, right, even if you're not sound feel like you're an executive in terms of your tone, and your mindset. You're a busy guy, you're an executive who wants to talk to another executive, your senior to the gatekeeper, and you just want to get to that person as quickly as possible. Kind of dismissive but not really dismissive, you don't want to have a dismissive or an arrogant tone. It helps, and it sounds silly but it helps if you pretend that you're writing, actually grab a pen and scribble on a piece of paper, while you're talking to this person, because that will be conveyed in the tone of your voice, that sense of, I'm busy, I'm senior to you I'm an executive and I need to speak to Bob, right now.

And that will come out in your voice, much better if you're actually pretending to be an executive, not claiming to be an executive, but in your mind, you're sitting there with a pen scribbling and just in your mindset, pretend that you're a senior executive, and you're just, you know, you just want to speak manager all our manager, to the gatekeeper's boss. So, what's this regarding just tell him it's regarding John Smith. Right, not arrogant, not dismissive, but a little bit busy. That's the steamroller approach, you want to be very careful with the tone of voice you use but that can definitely work.

Now another thing is to actually say that you're the executive. Now hopefully that's true, right, you don't want to say that it's not true. But if it is true, we'll then making it clear that you are an executive, let's say you're just, let's say it's just you, let's say you have a small business, a small b2b business, you and maybe a couple assistants, you're not a person on the sales floor making cold calls, you're the boss and you're making cold calls. The minute that you identify yourself, as the executive director of such and such or the managing director or the CEO of such and such company, you will have differentiated yourself, from the gatekeepers idea of salespeople. Does that make sense?

So, if they say, is he expecting your call, or what's this regarding, you can say just let him know that the CEO of such and such enterprises is calling. Just let him know that the managing director over at such and such as is calling and say with confidence like you're expecting in your mind psychologically you're expecting that that executive director is expecting to hear from you and will want to hear from you. Alright, a lot can be conveyed with tone, and for tone to be conveyed the right way you have to have that mindset, you have to have that mentality already. Another way to get around the expecting your call question, this one's a little bit iffy. Alright, it's not directly line but you can actually have a policy in your company, where everybody who needs to be called, has their name written on a sticky note, with the words call them, and slap that on the cold caller's desk, so that the cold caller you know can be with perfect honesty say when they're asked this question. Oh, I've got a note here, I've got a sticky note here saying that I'm supposed to call them. That sounds, it sounds a little bit iffy. Right, it sounds maybe a little bit deceptive. It's not technically a lie, but it might come in handy if that's the last straw, if that's the final thing that you just can't get past, that maybe consider doing that maybe consider literally having notes for the people, paper notes, for the people who you're supposed to call and then say, I've got a note here saying I'm supposed to call.

Next, you don't want to sound like an excited salesperson. Okay, now there's different schools of thought when it comes to actually selling. Right, you've got the more you know, restrained, refined to some people even call it an arrogant kind of approach to selling, where you don't sound very excited. It's kind of a reverse psychology kind of thing. And then you've got the hey be as enthusiastic and excited as you can, the car salesman kind of approach. And it doesn't matter which of those is correct, it doesn't matter which one you prefer. The thing to understand here and remember here is that you're not selling to the gatekeeper.

So, by no means, under no circumstances should you sound like a stereotypical excited, enthusiastic salesperson, you should not have your sales tone on when you're speaking to the gatekeeper. Because you might as well have a big sign on your forehead that says, I am a cold calling salesperson, protect your boss from me. So, it doesn't matter what your sales philosophy is, what you think is best for sales, doesn't matter, don't sound like a salesperson, on the phone, don't use either tactic on the phone, and definitely, this brings us to our next point. Definitely don't pitch to them, don't do it. There's this new idea out there that you should actually speak to the gatekeeper and say hey, can you tell me if you think this or that solution or offer would be a good fit for your company, I just want your opinion. And I'll tell you, it sounds pretentious, it sounds disingenuous, and it's probably going to bore the hell out of the gatekeeper. And the last thing they want to do is sit through it, now I'm not saying it can never work. I'm not saying that there isn't a way to do it, that doesn't sound pretentious, I'm not saying that there's no chance that you'll get lucky, and the gatekeeper will actually, you know, feel flattered and actually listen to you and give you, their opinion. And that might help you get through to the boss, not saying that that will never happen, but it is not a good idea to do that. You don't pitch to the gatekeeper; you need to get past the gatekeeper, and you have to remember that your job is to get past them and make your pitch to the decision-maker. So don't pitch to them, and that brings us to another point: we just keep it short and minimal. Okay, attention spans are incredibly low. In general, in life, so you only have like a 20 to 32nd window, to get your message across to the gatekeeper. So, make sure when you're practicing and typing up a script to make sure to keep that in mind as well. Keep it short and minimal, don't go into a long rambling explanation of why you want to talk to the decision-maker and so on and so forth, keep it short and minimal.

Next, and there's some debate about this, is humor, should you use humor, and the answer is maybe. That depends on your personality and your personal skill with humor. Alright, if you know that you're good at making jokes you know inserting a little bit of humor here and there to make the gatekeeper laugh or giggle, guess what, that's huge, that's golden if you can pull it off if you can get a gatekeeper to laugh, at something funny that you said. That is huge. You have made huge psychological inroads with that gatekeeper. The problem is if you tried to be funny and you don't succeed or then you'll do more damage than you would have if you were just not trying to be funny, so make sure you know yourself this is one of those know thyself situations can humor be used, absolutely. But only, only use it if you know you're good at it. And don't be silly, don't turn the whole thing into a comedy thing, we're talking about inserting something humorous here or there, a funny comment here or there, depending on the situation, where it sounds logical and reasonable and, you know, in some form of moderation. Okay, so humor is uh maybe depends very much on you, and just be careful with it.

Next up are compliments, compliments and we briefly touched on this idea a little bit earlier, but you can make the gatekeeper feel appreciated and respected if you pay some compliments as part of your intelligence gathering. Right, so when you're asking, you know who's in charge of this or that, or what time they come into the office or what time they leave the office. Well, you can pepper that or preface it a little bit, with something along the lines of, hey, you probably know more about what goes on there than anybody else. Right, you probably know the ins and outs of that place better than anybody, you know that's kind of a flattering thing to say. But you want to avoid a sense of pretentiousness or false flattery. So, this is something you gotta be really careful with, gauge the tone right, gauge the mood of the conversation. And make sure you deliver it in a very nonchalant way, okay because you can very easily turn this into something that actually sounds pretentious and disingenuous and attempt at false flattery, which makes the person feel like you're trying to manipulate them.

Right, so it'll actually have a damaging effect if you're not very careful, so use this sparingly, use it very carefully, and just be aware that it is a little bit risky. Now I mentioned earlier that a part of your intelligence collection, should include times, work hours, but not just the posted work hours, specifically, you want to know when the decision-maker usually shows up in the morning. And when they usually leave in the evening. Emphasis on the words usually you don't want the official numbers you want to know when they usually are there. And even better if you can figure out when the gatekeeper usually shows up, and when the gatekeeper usually leaves. If you can find out that information, it's golden. And the reason for that is because one of the best times to try and catch a decision-maker is before or after the gatekeeper has come to work, or left work because guess what, decision-makers executives business owners, they very often show up to work before anyone else. And they very often stay late after everyone else has left, has clocked out. And so that's a very, not very often talked about approach, it can be very effective. So, figure out what those times are, the unofficial times, the unofficial hours, and try to make contact during those hours. It's a very good chance that the person picking up the phone will be the boss will be the decision-maker, which can be very, very valuable if you handle it the right way.

Next, this is a very different approach. Instead of trying to get through the gatekeeper, try going around them, around them. What I mean by that is, there are certain departments that you can get put through to by the gatekeeper, that are not trained to be gatekeepers. And the gatekeeper is not trained to keep you away from.

So, if you call up and instead of saying hey, I want to reach the boss right and the gatekeeper immediately has their guard up their red flags are upright, it's time to do some gatekeeping, right, and instead you say they can you put me through to accounting I need to discuss something with accounting. Right, or people me through the shipping to the warehouse, can you put me through to, you know, the guys over in sales. Well, they're not trained to do any gatekeeping you're protecting of those departments. Those are boring departments, especially accounting, right then the warehouse. You're not going to get any resistance, in most cases from the gatekeeper, they're going to say, sure, let me patch you through to accounting. Right, or accounts receivable, or HR or even customer support, you just want to get on the phone with someone, in an office, maybe not customer support, because then they might actually send you through the customer support funnel, but any of those other departments, you actually get on the phone with someone else in another office who is not a gatekeeper who couldn't care less if you make it, to the decision-maker. And if you speak to them and start asking them questions, you can use that for intelligence collection. Right, ask hey who's in charge of such and such over there, who's the best person to talk to about this or that, what time does so and so leave, in the evening.

Right, you can ask questions like that. But you can also say, hey, can you patch me through, to Bill, which is your decision-maker. And it's very possible that some dude in accounting or in sales, or in the warehouse has no idea that he's supposed to be a gatekeeper, or that you might be a cold caller, or that the boss is not going to be happy with him, and he'll have the apparatus right there in his work phone, to patch you through, to the decision-maker. So, you can do that you can go around the gatekeeper by going through those so-called boring departments.

Those are avenues of attack that the gatekeeper is not expecting, anyone, to come through so their guard is not up there. The company's guard is not up in those places. And you can also use conversations that you had, with people in sales or in accounting, and you can use that as your icebreaker. Yeah, I spoke to Tom in accounting, and he said that you might want to hear about this, right when you're speaking to the decision-maker. So, you're starting off, on a note, that seems as though it's based on a legitimate conversation that you had earlier, and it is, if you had a conversation like that with one of those people in those boring departments, but more importantly it differentiates between, what they're hearing from you and the vibe, they're getting from you, and the usual feeling that they have about cold callers and salespeople. Now I know here about small talk. Small Talk can be okay. Now I know we said we want to keep it quick and concise, small, short, and minimalist. But there's going to be gaps, gaps in the conversation, there's going to be little periods of pause that are necessary, when the gatekeeper is doing something for you so let's say it's a receptionist and she says, sure, let me check his calendar. Right, let me look at the schedule and see if he's in a meeting, or maybe he's just going to poke his head around the corner, really quick, and see if you know so and so is in the office right now or pretend to see if so and so is in the office. Right any little gaps like those, are periods where it's okay to insert small talk, that's where you want to insert your small talk, your rapport building. Right, the no like and trust kind of stuff, you want to try your hand at some humor and get some giggles, that's fine, all that is okay during the gaps. Okay, so you want to keep the structure part of your conversation short, concise, quick to the point. But if there's gaps, it's fine to fill those gaps with some small talk. In fact, that is the ideal opportunity to do a little bit of small talk and some rapport building, and then so on.

Next, don't be afraid to be referred down. So, let's say that you, you can't quite get through the gatekeeper to the executive, but she's going to pass you through to someone at a lower level, maybe a middle-level manager. Right, or maybe you did get through to the executive, and you can tell right away he doesn't want to talk to you, but he is willing to pass you down the chain, to Steve, who's, you know, head of sales, right or something along those lines, or to Bill's assistant, you know, over in marketing.

Now just being real, yeah, it's true that that's probably not what you want, and it's not necessarily ideal, but it can actually be used to your benefit. Okay, so don't be afraid if you're getting referred down, don't give up. If you're getting referred down, you can actually say in a conversation to the next person that you're talking to that the boss has sent you. You can say, hey Bill, or hey, the executive director upstairs, said I should talk to you about this. He wanted me to have a talk with you about implementing such and such, you know, choose your wording carefully. But if you can, you know, spin it in a way that makes it sound and not inaccurately, this is actually accurate if you were referred down. If you can emphasize the idea, the vibe, the feeling, that the boss wants them to talk to you about something. Well, you can certainly do that, and sometimes even if that person at the middle level, let's say, is not able to make the buying decision. Sometimes they can book an appointment. Sometimes you can say they can you do me a favor, I really want to talk to Bob about this and it sounds like you're interested in, could you please talk to, you know, so and so via the receptionist or the executive assistant, and make sure that we get a date penciled in for a quick meeting with you, me, and Bob. Right, that's very possible, because now it's not just you trying to get the receptionist to get you a meeting booked. You got a mid-level manager, you got someone else in the organization who's trying to help you get that done, that's very useful, very useful. And it's also useful just in the sense of starting a conversation and planting a seed.

If the service that you provide, if the tool that you offer whatever it is that you're selling is actually really good. And especially if it's something that would be appreciated by, you know the mid-level folks or the underlings in the company, and you do a good job of explaining that to them. Well, guess what, if it's something that affects their day-to-day life gets rid of one of the annoyances that they have at work, guess what they're going to talk about it. They're going to mention it to their buddies, and they might even mention it to their boss, they might say to Bob hey, I really think you should, you know, hop on the phone with that one guy and buy that thing he's selling because that would get rid of XYZ problem that we have every day. I feel like we could sell, you know, 10 times as much paper if we had that tool that this guy is selling, man. You know you can actually plant real seeds like that and create demand for your product from within the organization, from the people at the bottom or the middle of the organization that can be really effective, really effective. So never ever be afraid to be referred down, it's not ideal, but it can definitely be turned and used to your advantage.

Now to sum all this up, the most important thing you can do here is prepare and practice. Get those common objections and your responses to those common objections ready, get those things ready, get those things memorized, or have them you know on a quick and easy to reference sheet in front of you, practice, practice, record yourself, listen to yourself. Use a partner roleplay with a partner, practice, practice, practice, but at the same time don't sound like you're reading from a script, don't sound like you're giving a memorized pitch. But if you're prepared before the call, and your practice, you're able to deliver smoothly. And you implement all these tips and tricks that we've just talked about, you could have a whole lot of success in cold calling, and it does not need to be something that you dread, and your success rate could absolutely skyrocket.

# Module 3

N ow in the next lesson, we're going to talk about those intelligence collection methods that we mentioned briefly earlier.

Alright, welcome to module three. In this module, our trainer will cover pre-call intelligence gathering, so get ready to take some notes, and let's jump right in.

Alright so the quick disclaimer, we're going to be looking at a bunch of tools and platforms here, and we do not have any association with those platforms, nor do they have an association with us, and you shouldn't assume that we are formally endorsing them or that they have any endorsement of us, we're simply pointing out some very useful tools that you can check out, to make the job of intelligence gathering for cold calling and specifically getting past the gatekeeper, a little bit easier. But the first one we're going to look at is LinkedIn Sales Navigator. This is a heck of a tool, for the b2b space. LinkedIn by itself is already pretty cool you can find out a lot about people and where they work, what position they hold, find out a lot about companies thought there's usually a little bit of a limit to what you can discover, based on your network size and how many degrees you're away from this person versus that person, and even the searches have limitations with a free LinkedIn account, but with LinkedIn Sales Navigator, you could do some serious deep searching to find out a whole lot about a whole lot of people, you can do searches that bring up all sorts of people with a specific role or responsibility or title, or in a specific industry. You can focus based on company size, you can get all sorts of potential leads from LinkedIn, and you can send them in mail messages. So, you don't have to be a connection of theirs in order to communicate with them. Now LinkedIn is great for that purpose alone, you can have some cold emailing or cold messaging success there. But in the context of cold calling, LinkedIn is great because you can send a message, and therefore have something to refer to, when you're speaking to the gatekeeper, to say that you're following up on this that or the other thing. So, LinkedIn Sales Navigator is great for reaching out, but also, it's great for gathering that intel, that intel on the people who work in companies, what roles they hold, which can be golden when you're trying to speak to the gatekeeper and use things like first names and knowing who the decision-maker is that you're trying to reach. So, LinkedIn Sales Navigator is definitely something to check out.

Another one here UpLead, UpLead as it says in the headline b2b prospecting with 95% data accuracy, they have some pretty good up to date databases of information here. A lot of databases that you'll have an across have some kind of outdated information. And that's, allegedly, not the case with UpLead. You can grab it names first name, last name, you can figure out what their title or their role is at the company and many times you'll even find things like direct phone numbers and direct emails for those people, which means potentially, depending on how good the information is you could skip the gatekeeper, but at a minimum, you can find out a lot about the people who work there, which you can refer to in your conversation with the gatekeeper, which, as we said is golden. So, this is a very cool tool that you could potentially invest in to help with your pre-called intelligence gathering.

Similar story here with Zoom info, Zoom info is a great way to get some good insights scoops on the companies that you're going after and the decision-makers you're trying to reach, same story as the previous one, you know, people's names, their role and title in the company, and in many cases a direct line, and a direct email to them, so great for gathering intelligence and as you can see they've won some awards in the past, this is a good reputable company that you can certainly check out and use them for your intelligence gathering need, another similar one here is Lucia for b2b contacts b2b leads, they've got a pretty good reputation. They claim to have at 1% accuracy, and that that is the highest in the industry, which is pretty impressive if it's true, and they are all good to go with the GDPR CCPA and other compliance issues that you might face when you're engaging in phone sales which is very important to keep in mind. They also give you some free contacts that you don't get charged for on a monthly basis, but once again same basic stuff as the other ones, you're basically getting access to a database that you can search filter and poke around and find names, positions, titles, and in many cases, direct lines, so very good stuff to have in your back pocket, before you pick up the phone and they get into a conversation with the gatekeeper.

Now this one is cool, Leadfeeder, this is not necessarily a database for reaching out and finding decision-makers and companies. At least that's not its primary purpose, Leadfeeder is able to tell you what companies have employees, visit your website. Okay, so it gets into the anonymous traffic that's visiting your website and it can identify when that traffic came from a company computer, and what company that was actually identifies which company had an employee come to your website, which of course, what's that mean? That means they're interested, or at least you can assume they're interested, and you can refer to that, when you're speaking to the gatekeeper when you finally call them, it has some cool automation and filtering that filters out ISP traffic and leaves you just with actual companies. Right, so this is purely b2b stuff that you're left with, and a good system for scoring and helping you figure out which ones you should prioritize, and you can search for decision-makers in their database, once you've determined that that company has, in fact, visited you. And boom, when you're talking to that gatekeeper you've got something to talk about, you can say hey so and so was interested in our such and such solution. And you're telling the truth because guess what, they visited your website, and you've got the proof right here. And so, this is a great, great, icebreaker, a great thing that you can say, or refer to when you're speaking to the gatekeeper and try to explain why you want to reach the decision-maker that you're asking for.

Finally, we've got RocketReach, which has a very large database as you can see 450 million professionals, across 17 million companies worldwide trusted by 7.9 million users, etc. And they've got, a search capability, they've also got a Chrome extension, so you can actually conveniently use that from within your browser when you're checking out a company or checking out listings for a company on LinkedIn or CrunchBase and so on and so forth. They've got lots of integrations to, you know, a connected to your CRM and all that good stuff. Obviously, it's working for sales, it works for other things as well, but we're interested in this one. Okay, trying to get good real-time up-to-date information, phone numbers, links to social media so you can learn more about the decision-makers that you're trying to reach, and so on and so forth. This is all just golden good information to have before you contact the company, and they get into a conversation with the gatekeeper.

Here's the deal, okay a lot of these companies just they all do the same thing. Okay, some of them might be better than others. Some of them might have bigger databases and others. The general idea is the same though, this is your chance to succeed where others fail because most people do not do pre-call intelligence gathering. Many of your competitors, skip that they're either too lazy to do it, or they're too, demotivated because we're tired of getting rejected by the gatekeeper, you know, they just want to get as many done in the day as possible and just get it over with and log in, you know, and clock out. If you take this seriously and do pre-call intelligence collection. Every time you're going to reach out to a decision-maker, you will be at a significant, significant advantage versus the competition, you will be able to differentiate yourself much better, and like we learned in the previous lesson, that's half the battle right there if you can differentiate you vastly increase the chances of getting through the gatekeeper into your decision-maker. So, take this aspect of the battle with the gatekeeper seriously collect intelligence before you make the call.

# Don't miss out!

Visit the website below and you can sign up to receive emails whenever B. Vincent publishes a new book. There's no charge and no obligation.

https://books2read.com/r/B-A-QWUO-EUNPB

BOOKS 2 READ

Connecting independent readers to independent writers.

# Also by B. Vincent

# About the Publisher

Accepting manuscripts in the most categories. We love to help people get their words available to the world.

Revival Waves of Glory focus is to provide more options to be published. We do traditional paperbacks, hardcovers, audio books and ebooks all over the world. A traditional royalty-based publisher that offers self-publishing options, Revival Waves provides a very author friendly and transparent publishing process, with President Bill Vincent involved in the full process of your book. Send us your manuscript and we will contact you as soon as possible.

Contact: Bill Vincent at rwgpublishing@yahoo.com www.rwgpublishing.com

.